Spreading Kindness

Being Kind Online

by Brienna Rossiter

FOCUS READERS.

PIONEER

www.focusreaders.com

Focus Readers is distributed by North Star Editions: sales@northstareditions.com | 888-417-0195

Produced for Focus Readers by Red Line Editorial.

Photographs ©: Shutterstock Images, cover, 1, 4, 6, 11, 13, 14, 16, 18, 20; iStockphoto, 8

Library of Congress Cataloging-in-Publication Data
Names: Rossiter, Brienna, author.
Title: Being kind online / by Brienna Rossiter.
Description: Lake Elmo, MN : Focus Readers, 2021. | Series: Spreading
  kindness | Includes index. | Audience: Grades 2-3
Identifiers: LCCN 2020033610 (print) | LCCN 2020033611 (ebook) | ISBN
  9781644936818 (hardcover) | ISBN 9781644937174 (paperback) | ISBN
  9781644937891 (pdf) | ISBN 9781644937532 (ebook)
Subjects: LCSH: Online social networks--Juvenile literature. |
  Kindness--Juvenile literature.
Classification: LCC HM742 .R673 2021 (print) | LCC HM742 (ebook) | DDC
  302.30285--dc23
LC record available at https://lccn.loc.gov/2020033610
LC ebook record available at https://lccn.loc.gov/2020033611

Printed in the United States of America
Mankato, MN
012021

About the Author

Brienna Rossiter is a writer and editor who lives in Minnesota. She loves cooking food and being outside.

Table of Contents

Chapter 1

Thinking of Feelings

People use the internet in many ways. They share pictures and videos. They send messages, too. They talk and write.

People don't always see who they are talking to. For this reason, people might not think about how others feel.

But thinking of others is very important. It helps you **avoid** hurting people's feelings.

Chapter 2

Kind Writing

Lots of online **communication** uses writing. But readers can't see the writer's face. And they can't hear the writer's voice. Sometimes this makes it hard to tell what the writer means.

When you write, choose words that are friendly and **polite**. Be extra careful about making jokes. People might not know you're trying to be funny. You could hurt their feelings.

Communicating Online

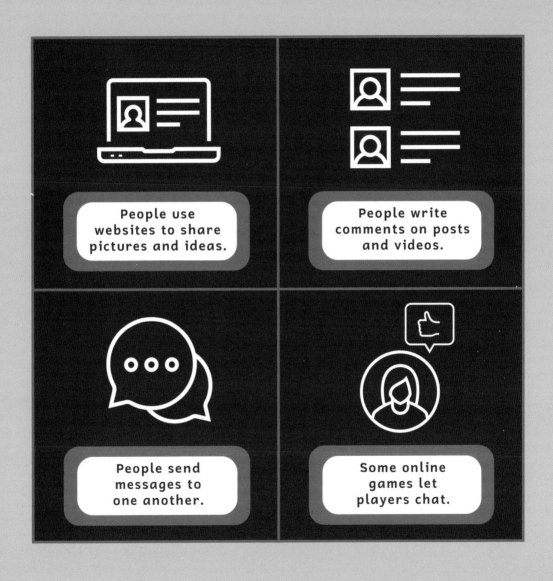

People use websites to share pictures and ideas.

People write comments on posts and videos.

People send messages to one another.

Some online games let players chat.

Read Before You Send

When you write online, start with a **draft**. Before you send it, read what you wrote. Think about how your message might sound to others. Make sure it is easy to understand. Change any words that sound rude or confusing. Read the message again. Then send it.

Chapter 3

Kind Posts

Stop and think before you post things. Once something is online, you might not be able to take it back. Plus, you might not get to choose who sees it.

Your post could be shared with many people. So, be careful what you post. Don't share posts that are angry or mean. Instead, show **respect** for others.

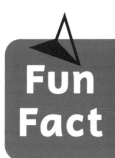

Fun Fact

Some posts go viral. They are shared by many people in a short time.

Chapter 4

Kind Words

Remember to be kind when you say things online. Treat others just like you would in person. Don't say mean things. And don't **gossip** about others.

Avoid getting into fights.

Be polite, even when people

disagree with you. If someone

says mean things, speak up.

Tell an adult. That way, you help

everyone stay safe.

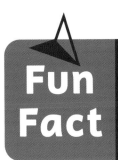

Fun Fact

Some people try to start fights online.

They are called trolls.

FOCUS ON
Being Kind Online

Write your answers on a separate piece of paper.

1. Write a sentence that explains the main idea of Chapter 3.

2. What is your favorite thing to do online? What do you like about it?

3. What should you do if someone says mean things to you online?
   A. say nothing
   B. say something mean back
   C. tell an adult

4. Why is it important to stop and think before posting?
   A. It helps your computer work faster.
   B. It helps you spot problems before it's too late.
   C. It makes people think you're smart.

Answer key on page 24.

Glossary

avoid
To try not to do something.

communication
A way of sharing news or ideas with other people.

draft
An early version that will be changed or improved.

gossip
To share unkind stories about other people.

polite
Showing good manners.

respect
Care for someone's thoughts and feelings.

To Learn More

BOOKS

Bassier, Emma. *Manners Online*. Minneapolis: Abdo Publishing, 2020.

Truesdell, Ann. *Respecting Others Online*. Ann Arbor, MI: Cherry Lake Publishing, 2020.

NOTE TO EDUCATORS

Visit **www.focusreaders.com** to find lesson plans, activities, links, and other resources related to this title.

Index

Answer Key: 1. Answers will vary; **2.** Answers will vary; **3.** C; **4.** B